T0170342

The Shimmering World

First Sentient Publications edition 2008
Copyright © 2008 by Steven Harrison and Richard Stodart

Cover design by Kim Johansen, Black Dog Design
Cover art by Richard Stodart
Book design by Connie Shaw

Library of Congress Cataloging-in-Publication Data
Harrison, Steven, 1954–
   The shimmering world : living meditation / by Steven Harrison. -- 1st Sentient Publications
ed.
       p. cm.
    ISBN 978-1-59181-066-7
   1. Life. I. Title.
BD431.H3145 2007
128--dc22

                              2007035246

Printed in China
10 9 8 7 6 5 4 3 2 1

SENTIENT PUBLICATIONS

A Limited Liability Company
1113 Spruce Street
Boulder, CO 80302
www.sentientpublications.com

The Shimmering World
Living Meditation

Steven Harrison

art by Richard Stodart
edited by Connie Shaw

SENTIENT PUBLICATIONS

This book is compiled from published and unpublished works of the contemporary mystic Steven Harrison. It is both an introduction to his work for those not familiar with him, and a collection of some of his most moving and penetrating statements for those who are. Its brevity and focus are intended to make it particularly useful as a tool for deep discovery. Please take these words to heart, sift them through the sieve of inquiry, and find clarity and fullness in the meditation that is your life.

—Connie Shaw, editor

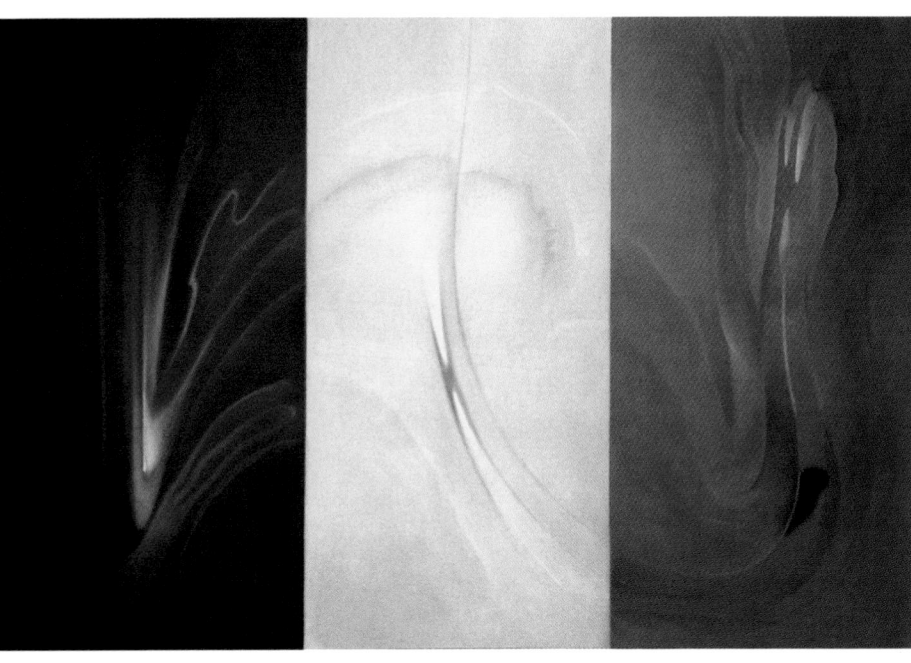

The question that life brings us is the movement of life itself, intrinsically dynamic, uncertain, and vital.

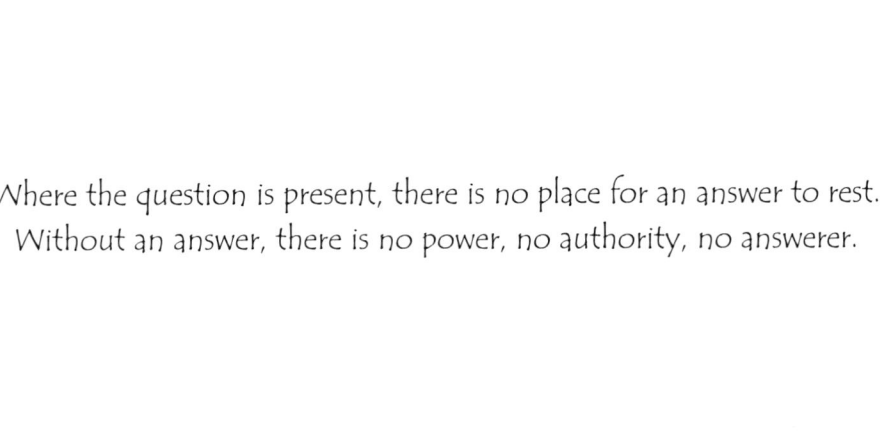

Where the question is present, there is no place for an answer to rest. Without an answer, there is no power, no authority, no answerer.

We are fascinated with the notion of understanding. We are sure the knowledge that we have accumulated through a lifetime of learning is very, very important.

It isn't.

It is very, very much in the way of direct perception. What we already know is static, but the life we seek to understand is not.

The spiritual teacher may provide us with the keys to the universe, but the universe is not locked.

The very grasping for an answer, for a response, for a solution that relieves us of the burden of feeling, is the problem. Without the grasping of the seeker, there is no solution. Without a solution, the nature of the problem fundamentally changes.

Humility is the absence of a particular position in relation to the world around us, the silencing of the critic within, the surrender to the movement of life without interpretation.

In the face of the vastness, the magic, the unknown quality of life, and in a moment of true humility, we may discover the actuality that washes away all our concepts.

In a wild moment of recognition, we look around at the world we inhabit and there is the primal experience of complete confusion. Confusion is the introduction to true intelligence – an intelligence without a center and without the dominance of thought.

We're lost in the woods. The worst thing to do is to wander around looking for the way out. Looking for a way out uses up our energy, makes us feel more and more frantic, and usually gets us even more confused and further from help.

The best thing to do when we are lost in the woods is to sit down, make a nice fire, and relax. The best thing is to wait for help to find us. If we're bored, we can make messages on the ground for airplanes to read.

We're lost in complexity. Looking for space in our life fills up the space of our life. It exhausts us and makes us feel more and more frantic and takes us further from help. Let the spaciousness of life find us.

It is always here, which is precisely where we are.

Relax. Help is very near.

We are in conflict. Stay with that fact. That conflict is vibrating; it is shaking our world. Let our world shake. Let it tumble down. Whatever is left standing is life itself. Life is not in conflict.

If we are prepared to look deeply at our conflict and not look away, we will discover that we are in a crisis of the spirit. Our life is on fire. Our life is falling away. Everything we have built and held dear is shattered. We have entered the dark night of the soul. We are prepared to die. And we are, for the first time in our lives, glimpsing freedom.

The spiritual crisis, when it visits our lives, is the moment of profound change. It is the moment when we may come to the root of our pain, the source of our existential dilemma. We do not need to fix it, we do not need to run from it, we do not need to fear it. We do not need to do anything. In doing nothing we are left with an acute awareness of all that is occurring. An acute awareness of all that is occurring is, after all, what we are.

Awareness is not the result of anything. There is nothing that causes it. There is nothing we can do to create it.

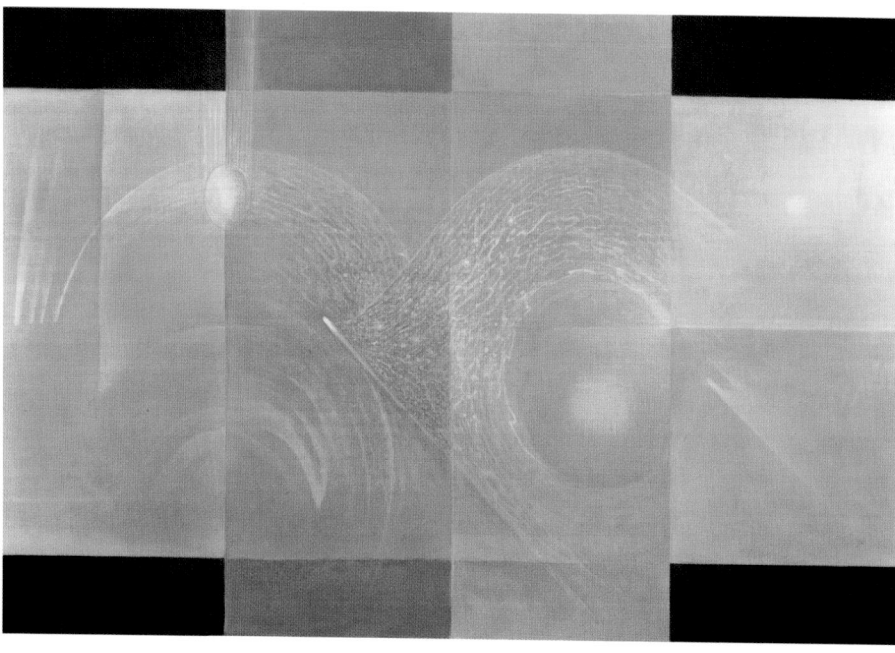

There is only one crisis, and it is a total crisis. The crisis is thought itself, our belief in it, our identification with it and with its bastard child, the "me."

We can do absolutely nothing about this "me." Doing nothing is not a technique. It can neither be taught nor learned. It cannot be practiced. The paradoxical hopelessness of the "me" realizing its own nature leaves us without an option, without a response, without a method. This stillness, without the possibility of action, without the hope for redemption, is the spontaneous realization of the truth of life.

By doing nothing we do not avoid what is happening. It is being described in the negative because it is not an action.
It is declining the action that avoids.

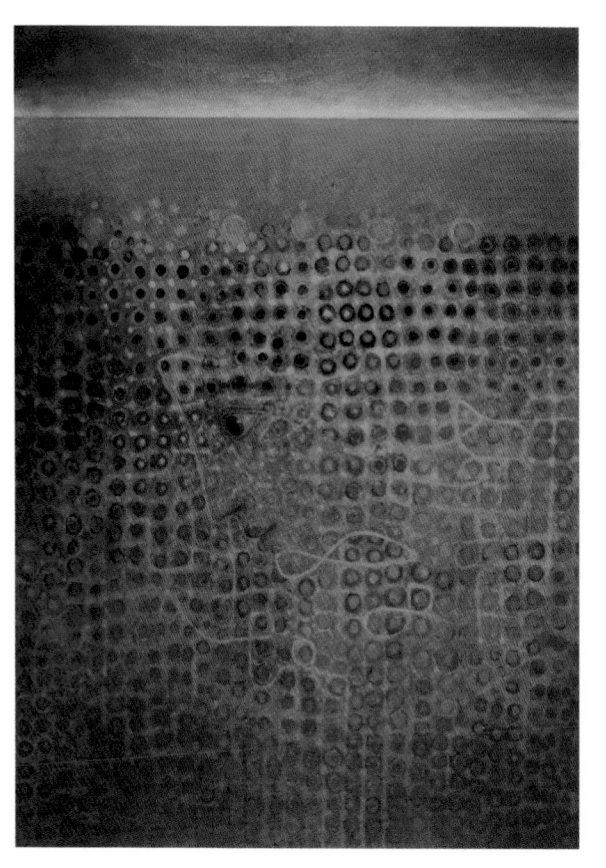

We feel conflict. We cannot turn to psychology to explain it. We cannot fix it. We cannot make it go away. The conflict we feel is not a problem. It is a messenger.

The conflict is existential. It is the friction between the bundle of ideas we call our self and the actuality of the boundarylessness of the world. We cannot learn to integrate; we can only discover that we are integrated. The conflict is the guide. If it is covered over, we lose our way to this discovery.

We do not need help; we need only understand that there is no choice in life but to follow the conflict where it takes us. If we are prepared to go there, we may discover the actuality of self and the nature of our sorrow.

The recognition of pain is the moment of freedom. Following this thread of conflict, we may come to the end of our difficulty by coming to the end of our selves.

It's not just that we don't have to change ourselves – it's that we *cannot* change ourselves. That realization is our freedom.

We may say that the world is illusion, but it is the viewer that is the illusion. The illusion is that the viewer is constant and solid.

The very nature of our existence is tenuous, hanging moment by moment, breath by breath on some invisible, evanescent quality called Life.

Death comes not just at the end of our life; it comes every moment. Look closely at the thought-body, at the mind as it creates reality through the arising of thought. Thought arises, but then it passes away. The universe is created and destroyed. Observe this carefully.

In the moment we die, in each moment we die, what is new is waiting to express.

Let the actual movement of life sweep through your life totally and you die, because there's nothing about the way you think of yourself that will survive that.

Is there a point of death, if there is no point of birth? If we cannot find a solid self in our minds or our bodies, then what is it that will dissolve in death? Is what we fear in death, the end of our separation, already a fact? What is not born cannot die. Death has already claimed that which is not actual.

Find the point of birth and at that moment death will be revealed. The alpha and omega are the same. That point of birth and death is this very moment, this very word, which falls away into absolute stillness. We know nothing about ourselves outside of the conditioned patterns. We don't know what our capacities are, or what our potential is. We don't know anything about ourselves other than that we are still, we are complete, and we are in relationship without need. We are no longer functioning in the context of life, but rather we are the expression of that context. The beauty of it is beyond description. It is beyond imagination.

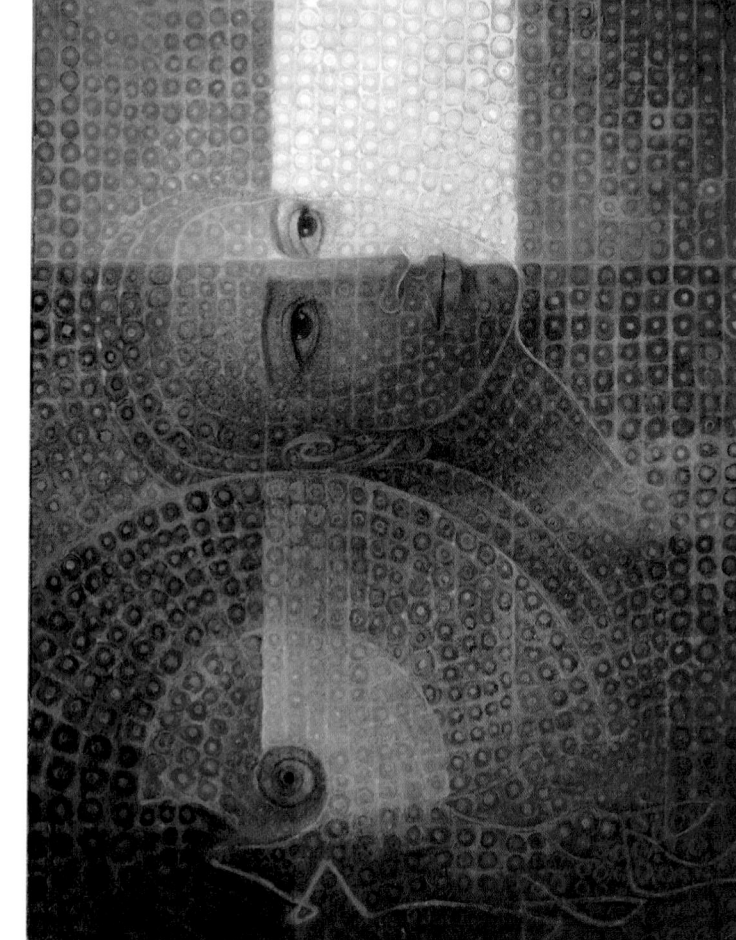

Change is the movement of energy without hindrance. It is the echo of life itself.

Change moves through us, through our habits, our resistance, our denial. Change is the truth of life.

Change is freedom. It is the end of attachment. It is the end of fear. There is nothing that binds us, there never has been.

The unknown is the portal to freedom. The life of freedom is fresh and vital simply because it is *not* the past, the repetition, the known.

Why does the unknown create such angst? The unknown is not really what it seems. It is not even unknown. What is truly unknown can generate no quality in our minds, because it does not yet have any quality. What is truly unknown cannot generate fear. What, then, is creating all of the fear by which we guide our lives?

Into the null set, the unknown, our minds project what fear tells us is there. This dark closet of our mind contains the memory of our failures, our hurts, our anxieties. This is the known, the repeating litany of the past by which we try to navigate the future. We cannot bear the thought of the unknown, not because it is empty, but because it is filled with our known. It is filled with us, and we are in pain.

Fear has looked hard at the life of freedom, feeling, and passion and declared it unfit for human habitation.

The fact is that fear is what is unfit for human habitation. Fear needs to be condemned and torn down. Yet we allow fear to operate our lives, and we live, with resignation, in the soul squalor of fear.

Love waits for fear to fall silent. Fear knows nothing about love and cannot know that love is waiting. Love is the greatest gift Fear will ever receive.

We think that if we can remove ourselves from stress, challenge, and difficulty, we will be happy. If we can rid ourselves of the screaming kid, the wife who doesn't look like she really loves us anymore, the mean boss, or the failing business, we will be happy. But we can't get rid of stress — life is inherently stressful. When we see that life is both stressful and dynamic, it's where we actually want to be *and* it's painful, then we can be happy. This is the full expression of life in this moment. There's no other place to go or be — the full texture of life is happening in the explosion out of this one moment.

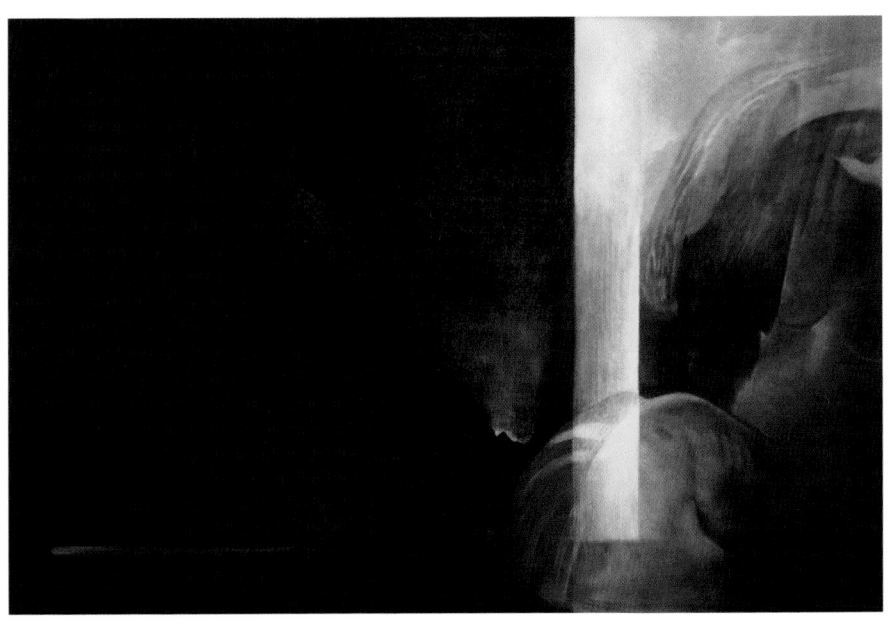

We are on the cutting edge, the brink, the edge of the abyss each and every moment. There are no guarantees to give and none to get. We are fully responsible for the entirety of our life.

Happiness grows only out of the profound silence in which the thoughts we call our self arise. In the moment our thoughts come still and just before the next thought arises – there, just there, is happiness. There, in the vast quiet, just there, is relationship.

Like archaeologists of the soul, we begin to uncover the debris of our mind. Our need to exist in full relationship to our world is what drives us. The layer upon layer of ideas, conditioning, and fear is what we dig through. In this search we have somehow forgotten that we have forgotten. The search has taken on a life of its own. The search has given us meaning that substitutes for what we have forgotten. But searching for love will not replace love. Nothing will replace love. If we forget everything else, let us remember that.

We know that we are both the teller of the tale and the expression of the story itself. We know that we are the meeting point of heaven and earth, the divine and the comic, the relative and the absolute. We can experience the divine in the depths of our humanness. We have the capacity to love.

છ

The hubris of knowledge must be the first sacrifice. For it, we get nothing in return. Nothing is a great gift indeed.

The world does not disappear in emptiness. It occurs in emptiness, and it is transformed by the recognition of emptiness.

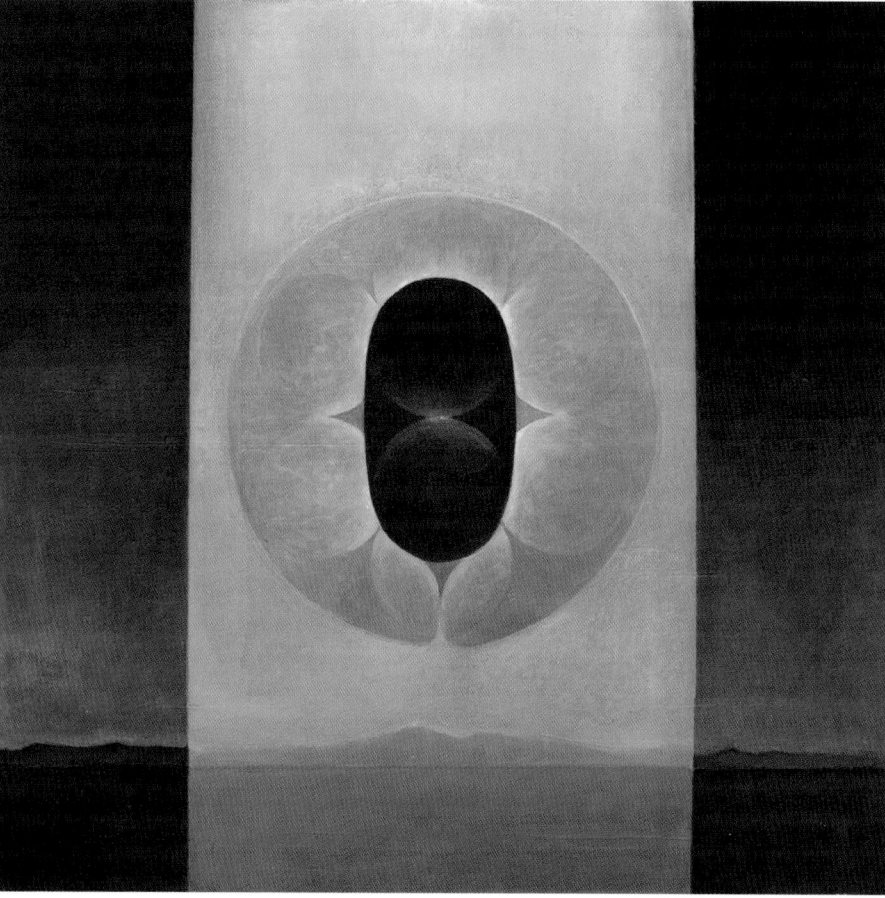

If we pay attention to the field of consciousness in which thought arises, we can find no separation. The field of consciousness is apparently boundaryless. This vast, undivided awareness is available to us at all times. It is there at any moment we are still. It is as present in us as our thoughts. But we identify with thoughts, which are limited and separating by nature. Why is it that we do not identify with the field of consciousness, the milieu in which these thoughts arise?

We can't find a self, a center, a "me," no matter how hard we try. We seem to be made up of, well, nothing.

Buddha was not just suggesting that we are nothing, he was pointing out that because we are nothing, we are everything. That's a lot.

We are terrified by the understanding that we are actually the universe. We are the power, the glory, the wisdom, the everything.

Jesus put the icing on the cake by directing us to love our neighbor as ourselves, which is about all we have left to do when we are nothing.

We are the human condition. And, knowing this, unavoidably we find compassion, connection, we fall in love.

We fall in love with ourselves, with each other, with the human condition.

Love, in the end, doesn't come from being loving. It comes from being human. It comes from our failure to love and from our fear of love. The mythic Jesus, after all, was incarnate as a human being. He had all the passions of a human and all the failures. In between some fairly impressive miracles, he perceived that the other is ourself. That's the miracle.

Love is the fire that burns us. We cannot survive; we cannot be there when something new emerges from the ashes, takes wing, and flies. This is why although we say we want love, in fact, we fear love.

The expression of love, all-encompassing, non-separate love, cannot be absorbed. It shatters the other as it shatters us. It is the most powerful and the most avoided energy. In love there is no "me." The parasite dies; the host lives.

Love is everything and, as such, cannot be contained by anything.

Love is a description of what is beyond words.

In love we are in relationship and, in relationship, everything is in contact with everything else, everything is part of everything else. We are not separate in love, and in truth, what we love is our separation. We cannot give it up, even though it is destroying us.

Aloneness is fearless. It is the ground on which we may enter into relationship with the world around us.
Aloneness has the integrity of needing nothing.

Aloneness is the transformer through which consciousness flows to become love. This love is the message of the universe. It is the truth of the universe. Yet, it cannot be touched by those who crave, who desire, who want. Only when we have found the absolute contentment of aloneness can we give expression to love. This is our purification.

All those who are inquiring stand alone in the universe. There is no reliable support, there is only our integrity as a guide. Even relationships forged in the understanding of this exploration, by their nature, must challenge, not coddle us.

Deep questioning of our existence is not for the fainthearted or the dilettante. Such exploration will disrupt, transform, and change the entirety of our perspective, because the perspective comes from a "me" that isn't there. This thin veil of illusion, once pierced, will always be pierced.

No one can give us directions on how to live with integrity. No one can certify that we are living our perceptions.

No authority can answer our question, but perhaps we will be fortunate and discover someone who will question our answer.

We stand alone, where we are. This is the portal to the whole of life.

The whole does not require us to figure it out, only that we live in the fullness of life. Our inquiry is not just the search for an explanation but the discovery of life itself in the actuality of each moment.

There is nothing outside of everything. All that we are left with is being. Being has no subject or object. It has no "thingness." Being subsumes everything. It is the universe as it is.

In being, there is only unity. It is the Self that the self forgot in early childhood. It is the love that we all seek in relationship to another. It is the mystic expression that religion seeks to convey.

In being, we discover our Self in relationship — not a relationship of time and space, but of two melded into one, self into Self, doing into being.

When we breathe, the universe breathes.

We saw in the beloved such promise, such beauty. We had such a direct experience of love, of expansion, of openness when we met.

We have only looked for this expanded feeling in another. We have never looked within our life as it is. We have never asked ourselves whether this vast feeling of connectedness, of safety, of surety, is available now, here, without anything, without another.

If this expanded feeling, this sense of love is not causative, if it does not occur because of something, then we are freed from the burden of acting, of doing, or searching. We do not need to find someone to give us love. We have love already. We are immersed in it. We cannot avoid it. The only way we can miss the fact of love is by searching for it, by looking for someone who can give it to us.

We are conditioned to this notion of another who will give us love. We believe with all our being that we have found love when we find the other. We have not found love. We have found a hopelessly flawed projection. We have found an impossible image. We have found an other who cannot possibly give us what we already have, what we have always had, and what we will always have. We have found the obscuration of our vision, the forgetting of our love, the overwhelming sleepiness of conditioning.

We have not found love. We have found contraction. We have shrunk the expansiveness of the universe into a bubble world consisting of me and the other. We become the center of the bubble, and all we see is a reflection of that center on the inner surface of the bubble. The shimmering world is perfect, it is just as we had hoped, it is all and everything. Then the bubble bursts.

One of the curses of human existence is the tendency to misconstrue language for actuality. Relationship has nothing to do with language, name, or concept. We cannot control relationship. We are already in relationship, but our view is so obscured that we do not recognize that fact.

If we are particularly alert, sensitive, and open, we may discover this fact. We are already in relationship.

If we have not discovered this, if we do not fundamentally experience this in our moment-to-moment existence, then we have fallen victim to the great curse. We are stuck in language, concept, thought. We are entombed in our own brains.

We are *thinking* our lives, not *living* them. We are thinking love and relationship, not living them.

The construction of thought in the face of the immensity of life is an absurd attempt to come up with a strategy. We think this rather pathetic attempt at construction is a plan that gives us safety and surety. Instead, it's the denial of the absolute power of life.

Thought has nowhere to go but its own isolated, endless, fragmented repetition.

Where are we going? We have nothing, which is what we have always had. There is no vantage point, but there is space. This space is not a concept (although we can try hard to make it one). It is empty of concept, empty of us.

This space transcends us, because it transcends our concepts. This space connects us, because in this space all actuality exists related not in a conceptual framework but in existential reality.

We have lost ourselves in nothing, and we have found our existence stripped bare of everything but its interrelatedness. We are not *in* relationship, we *are* relationship. In this moment we glimpse that this is the simple nature of what is. It has always been so, with or without our view or understanding.

This radically changes relationship to another, because we find no entry point to relationship and no exit from it. We cannot look for relationship; there is nothing to see that is not already in relationship. We cannot get anything from relationship; we already hold everything. We have no place to go and nothing to do.

When we come to love, we must throw out this last thing, this last idea. Whatever we call love, we must throw it out. Throw out the good feeling around the word; throw out the bad feeling for not having the word.

Throw out love. It is not actual. There is nothing that is love. Nothing is love. Love is nothing.

This is the frontier beyond which nothing can help us – no teacher, no theory, no philosophy, no book.
This is the space beyond language and beyond us.

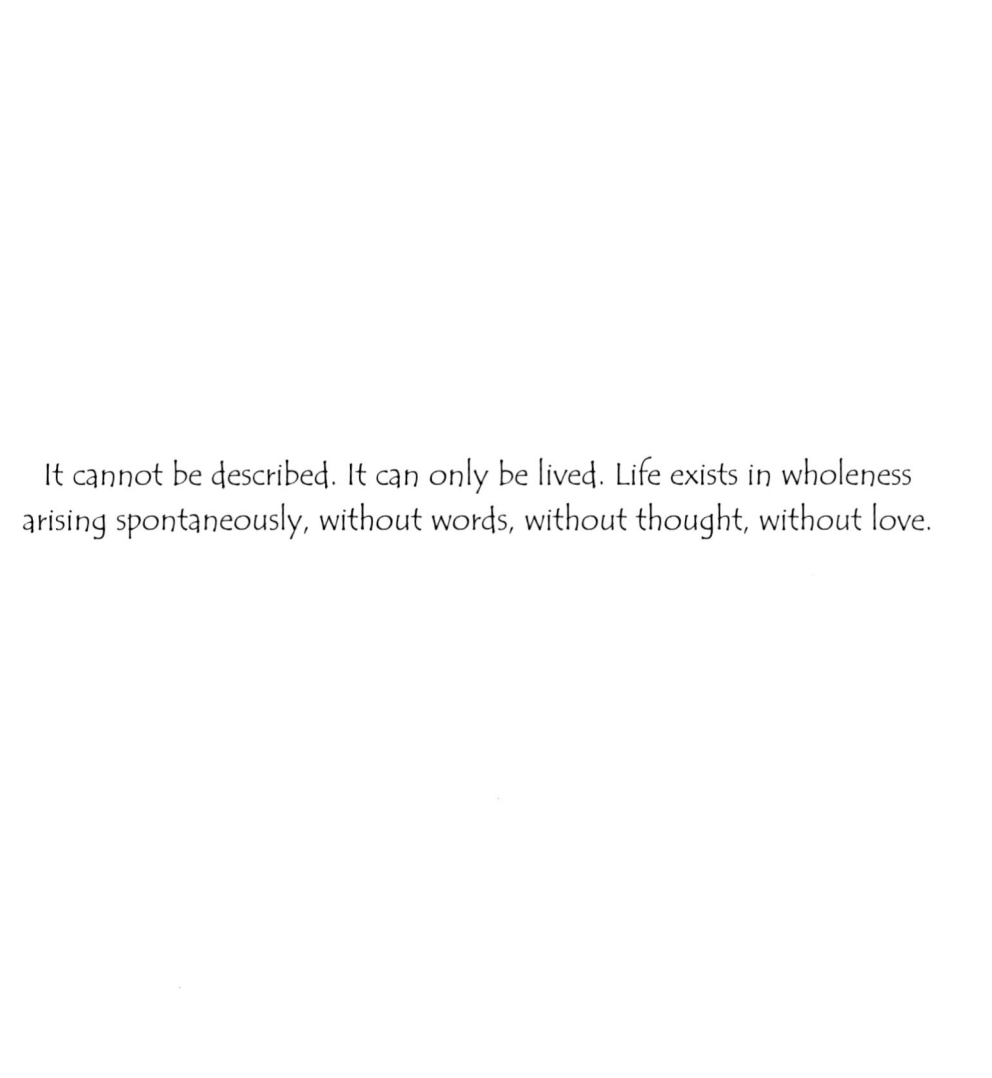

It cannot be described. It can only be lived. Life exists in wholeness arising spontaneously, without words, without thought, without love.

We have entered the realm of radical creativity where our art becomes the life we live, the forms we express, the very communication of the undivided energy we have discovered through the living experiment of our self.

We don't know anything about the creative space and that is the beauty, passion, and energy of it. That is why it's so alive.

Unless we reside within a belief system, we cannot find the criteria for failure. A life without authority puts us in direct contact with the effect of our life, our actions, our thoughts and feelings. Without the screen of belief we have direct perception of the world in which we exist.

How do we live without belief? We live without the conflict of my ideas with your ideas. We live without the competition of self with other. We live without resistance to the movement of life.

In the moment that we relinquish all authority, all conditioning, all projections of memory, both inner and outer, we are an empty vessel that is filled spontaneously with life itself.

❦

Walls that divide us from life take effort. Maintaining barriers requires energy. Openness is simple relaxation, letting go and giving up. The message of life will come through clearly in this state of openness.

The meditation of where we are is not even spiritual. It is life itself, moving of its own accord, fluid, quiet, beautiful, and self-fulfilled.

We live in the dynamic potential of existence, exploding in each moment, unpredictable, uncontrollable, and incredibly beautiful, and then fading into the profound silence of the universe. Faith is the recognition of the life force that animates this endless cycle of creation and decay.

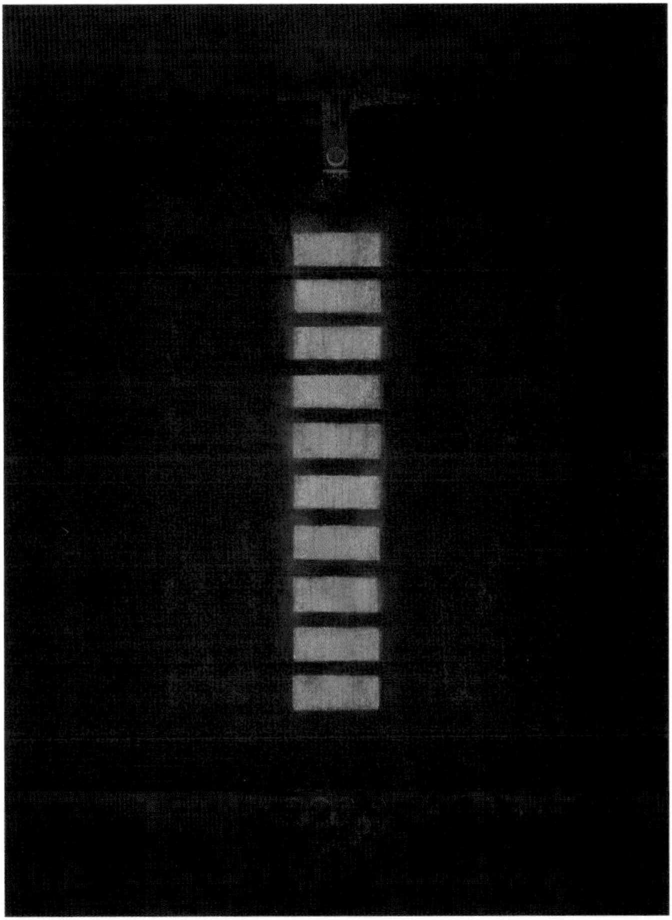

ABOUT THE AUTHOR

Steven Harrison is the author of *Doing Nothing, Being One, Getting to Where You Are, The Question to Life's Answers, The Happy Child,* and *What's Next After Now?*

ABOUT THE ARTIST

A native of Trinidad, the West Indies, Richard Stodart is a Canadian citizen and a graduate of Ryerson University in Toronto. He began painting in 1973 and in 1975 was awarded a Canada Council Grant for his paintings. Since 1976 he has lived in the United States.

The aim of Richard's work is to explore and present the freedom of dual and nondual unity. Many sources inspire him, including the spiritual teachings of Hinduism, Buddhism, Taoism, and Kabbalism.

Richard's art has appeared on magazine, book, and music album covers. His paintings have been exhibited in galleries in Canada, Hawaii, and the US mainland. He is the author of *Free and Easy Wandering, Markings on the Way*. Visit his website: www.richardstodart.com.

PAINTING TITLES

Cover

Title page

"The question that life brings..."

"When the question is present..."

"In a wild moment..."

"We're lost in the woods..."

"Awareness is..."

"By doing nothing..."

"It's not just that we ..."

"We may say..."

"The very nature of..."

"Change is the movement..."

"We are on the cutting edge..."

"The world does not disappear..."

"If we pay attention..."

"We can't find a self..."

"Jesus put the..."

Being and Acting as the Creative
Center of the Universe

Moon Over Trinidad

Trikaya

Full Moon and Clouds

Sky Dancer

I Ching

Demonstration of Great Order

Light Riddle

Emergence

Light Matrix

Sower's Seeds

She Wakens

Prometheus

Black Sun

Immortality

Chrystal Buddha

Transfiguration of Christ

"Love is the fire…"	Of an Ancient Civilization
"Aloneness is fearless…"	The Muse
"Aloneness is the transformer…"	Goddess of Purification
"When we breathe…"	Immortal Air
"We have not found love…"	Tiny Geometries
"When we come to love…"	Red Couple
"We have entered the realm…"	Immortal Water
"We live in the dynamic…"	Stupa

Sentient Publications, LLC publishes books on cultural creativity, experimental education, transformative spirituality, holistic health, new science, ecology, and other topics, approached from an integral viewpoint. Our authors are intensely interested in exploring the nature of life from fresh perspectives, addressing life's great questions, and fostering the full expression of the human potential. Sentient Publications' books arise from the spirit of inquiry and the richness of the inherent dialogue between writer and reader.

Our Culture Tools series is designed to give social catalyzers and cultural entrepreneurs the essential information, technology, and inspiration to forge a sustainable, creative, and compassionate world.

We are very interested in hearing from our readers. To direct suggestions or comments to us, or to be added to our mailing list, please contact:

SENTIENT PUBLICATIONS, LLC
1113 Spruce Street
Boulder, CO 80302
303-443-2188
contact@sentientpublications.com
www.sentientpublications.com